CONTENTS

Publishing Authority	3
Copyrighted and Intellectual Property Rights	4
All Rights Are Reserved	5
Dedication	6
In Service to a State, a Defense Force	7
Acknowledgment	8
Preface	10
Introduction	12
Disclaimer	14
Part One	16
Part Two	24
Part Three	31
Part Four	41
Part Five	53
Addendum Introduction	61
Addendum Part I	62
Addendum Part II	67
Addendum Part III	71
Addendum Part IV	75
Addendum Part V	79

Addendum Part VI	83
Addendum Part VI	87
Letter to the Reader	91
Glossary of Key Terms	94

Fior Publishers

STATE MILITARY INTELLIGENCE

BY

Hon. Daniel Bowen, 32°
Kentucky Colonel
Commonwealth of Kentucky
www.fiorpublishers.com

PUBLISHING AUTHORITY

Fior Publishers is a duly constituted publishing entity, authorized to conduct its business activities within the jurisdiction of the State of Alaska and throughout the United States of America. The publication herein has been issued by Fior Publishers in compliance with its governing authority, released on the 15th day of April 2024

Scope of Publishing Authority for Fior Publishers as Defined by the Relevant Industry Classification Codes:

NAICS 51-511130: Engaged in Book Publishing

NAICS 51-511199: Engaged in Miscellaneous Publishing Activities

NAICS 51-519190: Engaged in Other Information Services

These classification codes delineate the permissible range of operations for Fior Publishers and confirm its legitimacy in the various facets of the publishing and information services industries.

COPYRIGHTED AND INTELLECTUAL PROPERTY RIGHTS

This publication is constructed for educational purposes and is subject to the most permissive copyright limitations permissible under law. This volume aims to provide a comprehensive elucidation of legal, functional, and historical aspects of State Militias, both contemporary and historical, with a heavy focus on Intelligence and the purpose that community plays in the State Defense Forces than its antecedent works, collectively known as "State Armies of the United States."

The information contained within this scholarly work is intended for unrestrictive utilization by any parties interested in the subject matter. The publisher, Fior Publishers, reserves all rights to safeguard its proprietary information, intellectual property, and trademarks. The legal precedents and historical accounts contained within this educational material have been meticulously sourced from reliable authorities.

For any inquiries or requests pertaining to modifications, updates, or deletions of specific sections within this publication, please direct correspondence to Fior Publishers.

ALL RIGHTS ARE RESERVED

The reservation of specific rights related to this publication is governed by the Pan-American Copyright and Intellectual Property Convention. The book is structured for educational objectives and is subject to the most liberal copyright restrictions permitted by law.

As a consumer of the information contained within this publication, you are granted license by both the Author and Publisher to engage in the following activities, with exceptions only for trademarked and author-specific information:

Reproduction, Archival in a Retrieval System, Transmission, Re-transmission, Duplication, Scanning, Recording, Photographic Reproduction, and Photocopying The body of work within this volume.

This publication has been printed by Kindle Direct Publishing (KDP).

DEDICATION

To all who have served, those who serve today,
And to those whose service lies ahead.
Your sacrifice, service, and dedication
light up our way;
These grim halls filled with dark and grey.
You shall not be forgotten.

Hon. Daniel Bowen

This book is dedicated to you.

"It does not matter what they did while in the service, just that they served. While doing all they can, with honor, and dignity. Serving as a Cook, Cleaner, Infantry, Public Affairs, Police Officer, or Special Forces; service to the Country and its People is honorable service regardless of the job you had."

Col. Verdie Bowen
Director
State of Alaska
Office of Veterans Affairs

IN SERVICE TO A STATE, A DEFENSE FORCE

In the wild heart of Alaska, where the northern lights dance,
And the mountains stand guard, in their majestic stance,
There's a call that echoes, through valley and fjord,
A call to serve, in the Alaska State Defense Force.

Not for glory, nor for fame, do these brave souls fight,
But for love of their land, under the aurora's light.
With hearts ablaze, and spirits fierce and bold,
They stand ready, their story to be told.

It's a call to the valiant, who see beyond the self,
To those who place service, above all else.
With courage as their compass, and honor as their guide,
Beside the mighty eagle, they stand with pride.

This is the land of the free, because of the brave,
Who vow to protect it, from crag to wave.
In the chill of the winter, or the summer's mild grace,
They are the guardians, of this wild place.

So let the fire in your heart, be kindled with desire,
To join the ranks, and to aspire,
To serve where the midnight sun meets the sea,
In the Alaska State Defense Force, be all you can be.

For in this service, you'll find more than a role,
You'll find a purpose, a part of your soul.
In the land of the pioneers, let your legacy be,
One of service, of honor, of making history.

Answer the call, let it not go in vain,
For Alaska's beauty, is not without pain.
Be the shield in the storm, the light in the dark,
In the Alaska State Defense Force, leave your mark.

Honorable Daniel Bowen, 32°
Published in:
Echoes of Time - Poetic Musings by a Kentucky Colonel

ACKNOWLEDGMENT

As I reflect on the journey of writing "State Military Intelligence," my gratitude extends to many who have influenced and supported this endeavor. I am profoundly indebted to my parents, Colonel Verdie Bowen and Colonel Catherine Bowen, for their foundational support which has been a cornerstone of my personal and professional life.

My deepest appreciation goes to my wife, Andrealaine Bowen, for her endless patience and steadfast support through the countless hours of research, writing, and revision that this book demanded. Her encouragement was vital in bringing this project to fruition.

I am grateful for the opportunity to serve under the exceptional leadership of Brigadier General Simon Brown II, Commander of the State of Alaska's 49th Brigade State Defense Forces, and Lieutenant General Torrence Saxe, the Adjutant General of the State of Alaska Organized Militia. My involvement with the 49th Brigade has been deeply enriching and was made possible through a Warrant to the rank of Warrant Officer, a privilege granted under the authority of Lieutenant General Saxe and executed by Brigadier General Brown.

A heartfelt acknowledgment must also go to M.E. Bolin for her mentorship and guidance during my time at the U.S. Department of Homeland Security,

Office of Behavior Detection and Analysis. Serving under her leadership and having the opportunity to instruct in Behavior Detection and the Analysis of human behavior has profoundly shaped my professional path and this book's perspective on intelligence analysis.

Special thanks to Colonel John James, Commander of the State of Alaska 49th Brigade State Defense Forces Second Scout Battalion, for his leadership and inspiration. May your vigilance continue to fortify our defenses.

Lastly, I extend my gratitude to the Commonwealth of Kentucky for honoring me with a Commission and the distinguished title of Kentucky Colonel.

To everyone mentioned and all those who have walked this path with me, your collective influence has been a beacon of inspiration. Thank you for your unwavering support and belief in my work.

PREFACE

Good day,

I am the Honorable Daniel Bowen 32° (Kentucky Colonel), and my journey continues through various roles that not only define my professional ethos but also reflect my commitment to serving our nation and its communities. Among these, I am a Colonel of the Commonwealth of Kentucky, an Honorary Governor's Aide De Camp, a Published Author, a Freemason, a Borough Politician, a Federal Employee, and a devoted Son, Brother, Husband, Father, Friend, and State Soldier.

Currently, I serve as a Chief Warrant Officer in the 49th Brigade Headquarters, Alaska State Defense Force, specifically within the S-2 Section. My tenure as a former master certified Officer and former instructor with the United States Department of Homeland Security's Office of Behavior Detection and Analysis has equipped me with unique insights into the intricate world of behavior analysis and intelligence operations. These experiences have been instrumental in shaping the narrative of this book.

"State Military Intelligence" is born from my extensive involvement in intelligence gathering and analysis, both in a federal capacity and within the framework of the State Defense Forces. This book is designed to unfold the complex tapestry of intelligence operations at the state level, providing a detailed examination of the legalities and ethical considerations that underpin these activities in order to break down the information into a simple and easy to read format.

The impetus for this volume, much like its predecessors, stems from a desire to illuminate the often opaque realms of state-level intelligence and militia and its crucial role in safeguarding public safety. Here, I bring together pieces of knowledge, from legislative texts to operational experiences, aiming to offer readers an easier and simple understanding of how intelligence functions within State Defense Forces and its broader implications for national security; this includes additional details on what intelligence is and how it is gathered through the most simplest of terms.

Whether you are a professional within the military or intelligence communities, a policy maker, or simply a citizen intrigued by the strategic underpinnings of state security, this book aims to enrich your understanding and appreciation of the essential balance between maintaining security and upholding the freedoms we cherish.

Yours sincerely,

Hon. Daniel Bowen, 32°
Kentucky Colonel

INTRODUCTION

In a world where information is as crucial as physical assets for national and regional security, the strategic importance of intelligence within State Defense Forces (SDFs) cannot be overstated. This book offers an examination of the integral role and capabilities of SDFs, with a specific focus on their intelligence operations. It navigates through the legislative frameworks that govern these forces, delves into their historical contexts, and unveils the sophisticated realm of intelligence gathering, from Open-Source Intelligence (OSINT) to Human Intelligence (HUMINT).

The initial parts set the stage by defining what State Defense Forces are and exploring the legal and historical underpinnings that have shaped their current roles within the United States. Following this foundation, the book progresses into the core of intelligence, explaining its principles and the methodologies employed in effective information analysis. Subsequent parts provide a deep dive into the specific intelligence capabilities of SDFs, highlighting the tools and techniques used in OSINT and HUMINT to enhance state-level security and disaster response.

A crucial aspect of this analysis is the exploration of how SDFs integrate their intelligence functions with other branches of state military components, such as the National Guard and Naval Militia, to create a cohesive and efficient defense ecosystem. Best practices and strategic applications of intelligence are discussed, demonstrating how these can empower state governments to make informed decisions and respond adeptly to both threats and emergencies.

Concluding with a synthesis of insights and forward-looking perspectives, this book aims to serve as an authoritative resource for military officials, policymakers, and academics interested in the optimization of intelligence functions within State Defense Forces. It is an essential guide for enhancing understanding and efficacy in the crucial intersection of intelligence and state-level defense.

DISCLAIMER

This book discusses the structures, roles, and functions of intelligence gathering and analysis within the context of State Defense Forces. It is important to emphasize that the intelligence operations described herein are strictly governed by legal and ethical guidelines designed to protect the rights and privacy of citizens.

The intelligence activities of State Defense Forces are not to be utilized for surveillance or any form of intelligence gathering against citizens of the United States or its territories. These activities are regulated under various laws and statutes to ensure they uphold the constitutional rights and freedoms of individuals.

Scope and Purpose of Intelligence Use

The primary purpose of intelligence gathering and analysis by State Defense Forces is to aid in disaster preparedness and response, and to provide insights into foreign threats against the United States. This includes monitoring global events and trends that may impact national security or require a coordinated response from civil authorities. Intelligence efforts are focused on external threats and operational planning for homeland defense, rather than domestic surveillance.

All intelligence operations conducted by State Defense

Forces must comply with federal and state laws, including but not limited to the U.S. Constitution, the Posse Comitatus Act, and other relevant legal frameworks that prohibit military involvement in civilian law enforcement, except under expressly authorized circumstances. These operations are conducted with the utmost respect for the law and for the rights of all individuals.

When State Defense Forces are called upon to support civil authorities, whether in response to natural disasters, emergencies, or security operations, intelligence gathering and analysis are used solely to enhance the effectiveness and efficiency of the mission. This is aimed at ensuring public safety and coordinating response efforts that benefit affected communities.

This disclaimer serves to clarify the intent and limitations of the content presented in this book regarding the use of intelligence by State Defense Forces. It underscores our commitment to ethical conduct, adherence to legal standards, and the respectful treatment of all individuals' rights and privacy.

PART ONE

The United States stands as a monumental experiment in governance, born from a constitution that enshrines the balance of power and the safeguarding of liberties. Integral to this balance are the State Defense Forces (SDFs), which are rooted in the earliest legal documents of the nation. This part explores the constitutional legislative, and historical frameworks that establish and regulate these forces, underscoring their importance in national defense and state security.

Legality of State Defense Forces

The U.S. Constitution is not merely a document outlining the structure of government, but a framework designed to limit governmental powers and protect individual freedoms. Historical figures like George Washington and John Adams emphasized the necessity of this framework while acknowledging its imperfections and the need for a moral citizenry. Benjamin Franklin's adage that nothing in the world is certain "except death and taxes" humorously belies the serious endeavor of creating a lasting democratic system, which includes provisions for a militia.

The framers of the Constitution were deeply wary of a standing federal army, which they viewed as a potential tool of oppression. They envisioned the militia as a democratic force, a bulwark against tyranny. Composed of civilian soldiers, the militia would protect the nation and ensure that military power remained under civilian control, as reflected in their writings and the constitutional text.

The term "militia" in the United States encompasses the National Guard "Organized Federal Militia", the State Defense Forces "Organized State Militia", the Naval Militia "Duel Federal and State Organized Militia", and the Air Force Militia "Organized State Militia". Each component serves under different legal frameworks, with the National Guard operating under both state and federal control, while SDFs remain strictly under state jurisdiction unless federalized by Congress.

Key constitutional provisions relevant to the SDFs include:

Article I, Section 8, Clauses 11-16: These clauses empower Congress to raise and support armies and to provide for organizing, arming, and disciplining the federal and state militia.

The Second Amendment: This amendment protects the right to keep and bear arms and mentions a "well-regulated Militia" as being necessary to the security of a free state, underpinning the existence and regulation of state militias.

These provisions delineate the powers shared between the state and federal governments concerning military forces, ensuring a balance that prevents the concentration of military power.

The Militia Act of 1792 set the early standards for what would become a more defined system under subsequent laws, including the National Defense Act of 1916, which more clearly divided the roles between the National Guard and the SDFs. Modern frameworks are primarily found in Title 10 and Title 32 of the United States Code, which outline the roles, duties, and rights of these forces, ensuring they are well-regulated and equipped to serve.

While federal laws provide the framework and federal authorization, states have significant latitude to regulate their militias in accordance with the federal constitution. For example, Alaska's statutes not only provide for the Alaska National Guard but also for the Alaska State Defense Force, illustrating how state laws can reflect specific local needs and complement federal standards.

SDFs have proven their value repeatedly, responding effectively to natural disasters, supporting law enforcement during civil unrest, and enhancing homeland security. These forces exemplify the citizen-soldier ethos, providing a vital link between the military and civilian spheres and reinforcing the principles of community and state resilience. They embody a critical aspect of American military and civic structure and are a manifestation of the foundational American principles of democracy, state rights, and civic responsibility. Understanding their constitutional basis is essential for appreciating their role in contemporary society, ensuring that as challenges evolve, the framework governing these forces remains robust and responsive.

Brief History of State Defense Forces

The history of State Defense Forces (SDFs) in the United States is a narrative deeply intertwined with the nation's founding principles and its evolving defense needs. This next section of the part explores the origins, evolution, and pivotal moments in the development of SDFs, providing a comprehensive backdrop to their current role and significance.

The concept of a militia in America predates the formation of the United States, rooted in the early colonial period when citizens organized themselves to defend their communities against various threats and from European invaders. This civilian-based defense ethos was deeply ingrained in the American spirit and was a precursor to the modern State Defense Forces.

The militias played a crucial role during the American Revolution, fighting against British forces and serving as the primary military force of the nascent nation. After the revolution, the framers of the Constitution incorporated the militia into the national defense strategy, acknowledging its importance while also recognizing the potential dangers of a standing army, as reflected in the thoughts of President John Adams and the English Bill of Rights 1689.

The Militia Act of 1792 formalized the role of the militia, requiring all able-bodied men to enroll in the local militia and defining how these units would be organized and called into service. It laid the groundwork for a national defense strategy that included both a regular army and a citizens' militia, the latter of which evolved into today's National Guard and State Defense Forces.

Throughout the 19th century, state militias faced numerous challenges, including varied participation rates and inconsistent training standards especially during the War of 1812 and the Mexican American War. These challenges prompted reforms that gradually transformed state militias into more organized and reliable units.

The early 20th century, particularly the periods during World War I and World War II, marked significant turning points for state militias. They were federalized to supplement U.S. military forces, serving in both combat and support roles. The National Defense Act of 1916 and subsequent legislation redefined the militia, creating the National Guard as the primary organized federal militia force and paving the way for the modern State Defense Forces detailed in federal statute as the organized state militia force.

During the Cold War, the role of SDFs shifted toward civil defense, preparing for, and managing potential disasters, both natural and man-made. As threats evolved, so did the functions of the SDFs, expanding to include disaster response, emergency management, and, more recently, cybersecurity.

Today, State Defense Forces are legally recognized under Title 32 of the United States Code, which allows states to maintain their own military forces separate from the National Guard. Each state has the authority to define the structure, role, and mission of its SDF, which can vary significantly from one state to another. The primary role of SDFs remains the same, serving their state in a military role, especially during emergencies when the National Guard is deployed federally or when the nation needs a trained military force to repel an invasion or end an insurrection.

The history of State Defense Forces is a testament to the enduring value and adaptability of state-level military organizations in the United States. From their origins in the colonial militias to their current status as key components of state and national emergency response frameworks, SDFs continue to play a vital role in public safety and civil support. Understanding their historical context enriches our appreciation of their function and ongoing relevance in contemporary security and defense strategies.

Here are just a few quotes to sum up this part to help

facilitate a better understanding and appreciation of the State Defense Force History:

"The militia is composed of free citizens. There is therefore no danger of their making. Use of their power to the destruction of their own rights or suffering others to invade them. I earnestly wish that young gentlemen of a military genius, and many such I am satisfied there are in our colony, might be instructed in the art of war, and taught at the same time the principles of a free government, and deeply impressed with a sense of that indispensable obligation which every individual is under to the whole society. These might in time be fit for officers in the militia and being thoroughly acquainted with the duties of citizens as well as soldiers might be entrusted with a share of command of our army, as such times necessity might require so dangerous a body to exist." - United States President John Adams

"And thereupon the said lords spiritual and temporal and commons, pursuant to their respective letters and elections, being now assembled in a full and free representative of this nation… that the raising or keeping a standing army within the kingdom in time of peace, unless it be with consent of parliament, is against law." - English Bill of Rights 1689

"Before a standing army can rule, the people must be disarmed; as they are in every kingdom in Europe. The supreme power in America cannot enforce unjust laws by the sword; because the whole body of the people are armed and constitute a force superior to any bands of regular troops that can be, on any pretense, raised in the United States." – Noah Webster

PART TWO

In an era where information is a prime asset for security and governance, the intelligence operations of State Defense Forces (SDFs) walk a fine line between safeguarding the public and respecting individual privacy and civil liberties.

This part delves into the complex interplay between national security needs and the rights of citizens, exploring the ethical frameworks that govern SDF intelligence activities, the challenges they present, and potential strategies for balancing security with civil liberties.

To understand the balance of privacy and intelligence gathering, it's crucial to start with the foundational legal frameworks that govern these activities.

The U.S. Constitution: The Fourth Amendment protects citizens against unreasonable searches and seizures, a principle that extends into the realm of digital and data privacy. The interpretation of what constitutes "unreasonable" in the age of digital intelligence is a subject of ongoing legal debate.

The Posse Comitatus Act: This 1878 law limits the powers of the federal government in using federal military personnel to enforce domestic policies and is often cited in discussions about the military's role in domestic intelligence operations.

State Laws and Regulations: Each state may have its own set of laws that further define and restrict the operations of its SDF, particularly concerning intelligence operations within its borders.

As SDFs employ various forms of intelligence gathering, several challenges arise in balancing these efforts with the need to protect civil liberties.

Data Overreach

Issue: The collection of data beyond legitimate security needs can infringe on individuals' privacy rights. This overreach can occur when intelligence operations collect vast amounts of data indiscriminately without specific targets or defined purposes.

Impact: Indiscriminate data collection can lead to the misuse of personal information, potentially leading to unauthorized surveillance and violations of privacy.

Solution: Establishing strict operational limits that clearly define the scope and purpose of data collection efforts. This includes setting stringent criteria for the types of data collected and the conditions under which it can be gathered.

Technology and Surveillance

Issue: Rapid advancements in technology provides tools that can collect data extensively and intrusively. For example, cell phone tracking can reveal personal movements and habits, drones can collect detailed aerial images, and facial recognition technology can identify individuals in public spaces without their consent.

Impact: The use of these technologies without proper guidelines can lead to a surveillance state where citizens' movements and actions are constantly monitored, undermining personal freedoms and privacy.

Solution: Implementing strict guidelines and regulatory frameworks that govern the use of surveillance technologies. This includes ensuring that their use is justified, proportional, and accompanied by appropriate safeguards to protect privacy.

Information Sharing

Issue: Intelligence sharing between different agencies and jurisdictions can result in the spread of personal information beyond the original purpose for which it was collected, potentially leading to privacy breaches.

Impact: Without proper controls, information sharing can lead to the exposure of sensitive personal data, risking misuse and unauthorized access.

Solution: Establishing formal agreements and protocols that define what information can be shared, with whom, under what circumstances, and how it should be protected. These agreements should comply with legal standards and respect individuals' privacy rights.

Ethical Implications and Debates

The Right to Privacy vs. the Need for Security

Debate: Balancing the individual's right to privacy with the state's need to ensure security is a fundamental challenge. This debate often centers on the extent to which it is acceptable to encroach on personal privacy in the interest of national or state security.

Discussion Points: Consideration of whether the security measures in place are proportional to the threat and whether less invasive alternatives have been considered. The debate also involves examining the long-term implications of eroding privacy rights for security purposes.

Oversight and Accountability

Issue: There is often concern about whether existing oversight mechanisms are sufficient to prevent the abuse of intelligence powers. Questions arise about the effectiveness of internal controls and whether external oversight by independent bodies is adequate.

Solution: Strengthening oversight mechanisms by involving judiciary oversight through warrants, enhancing congressional or parliamentary scrutiny, and ensuring transparency and accountability in intelligence operations.

Bias and Discrimination

Issue: The use of algorithmic tools in intelligence gathering can inadvertently lead to biased outcomes, particularly if the algorithms are trained on skewed data sets.

Impact: Such bias can result in discriminatory practices, where certain groups may be unfairly targeted or disproportionately affected by surveillance and enforcement actions.

Solution: Implementing measures to ensure that algorithmic tools are developed and used in ways that are fair and unbiased. This includes regular audits of algorithms for bias, involving diverse teams in the development of technology, and establishing ethical guidelines for the use of artificial intelligence.

Frameworks to Address Challenges

Clear Operational Guidelines:

Establish detailed protocols for each type of intelligence operation, clearly defining what is permissible and what is not. Guidelines should also cover the methods of data collection, analysis, storage, and deletion.

Regular Audits and Oversight:

Regular audits by independent oversight bodies can ensure that intelligence practices adhere to legal and ethical standards. These audits should assess both the legality of the operations and the safeguarding of civil liberties.

Transparency and Public Engagement:

Engaging the public through transparent practices builds trust and ensures accountability. This includes releasing reports on the nature and results of surveillance activities (within the limits of security) and publicizing the safeguards in place to protect civil liberties.

Technology-Specific Policies:

Creating specific policies for each type of technology used in intelligence operations ensures that their deployment does not infringe on civil liberties. Policies should govern the acquisition, use, and limits of technology such as drones, facial recognition, and data analytics tools.

By addressing these challenges and ethical implications through robust frameworks, SDFs can ensure that their intelligence operations are conducted responsibly, respecting both the security needs of the state and the civil liberties of its citizens.

As State Defense Forces continue to play a critical role in state-level security operations, balancing these responsibilities with the privacy and civil liberties of citizens has never been more critical. By establishing and maintaining robust legal and ethical frameworks, ensuring rigorous oversight, and fostering a culture of transparency and accountability, SDFs can protect both the security and the freedoms of the communities they serve. This delicate balance is not only essential for the legality and legitimacy of intelligence operations but also for maintaining the public trust, which is fundamental to the operational success of SDFs in their security missions.

PART THREE

Before we delve into how the intelligence apparatus interacts and compliment the State Defense Forces, let us learn what intelligence and the analysis of intelligence is.

Intelligence, in its broadest sense, is a critical resource that informs decisions, shapes strategies, and secures nations. In the context of military and defense operations, the role of intelligence is multifaceted, influencing everything from tactical decisions on the battlefield to strategic policymaking at the highest levels of government. This part delves into the fundamental concepts of intelligence, exploring its definition, scope, and the various types it encompasses.

Military intelligence refers to the collection, analysis, and use of information that supports commanders in their decisions. It involves not only the tactical aspects of identifying and countering immediate threats but also the strategic side of foreseeing long-term geopolitical shifts. The scope of military intelligence is extensive, covering a wide array of activities, including the monitoring of adversaries, the protection of friendly forces, the assessment of environments, and the planning of operations. Effective intelligence operations can mean the difference between victory and defeat, making it a cornerstone of national security.

Intelligence gathering can be categorized into several types, each with its specific methods and purposes. These include:

Signals Intelligence (SIGINT): This involves intercepting signals between people, such as phone calls and emails, or signals emitted by devices like radar or weapons systems. SIGINT is crucial for understanding the capabilities and intentions of adversaries by eavesdropping on their communications or electronic signals.

Human Intelligence (HUMINT): HUMINT is gathered from human sources. This can involve espionage, where trained agents gather covert information, or the debriefing of refugees, defectors, and prisoners of war. HUMINT is often portrayed as the most direct form of intelligence, as it involves actual interaction with sources to obtain data.

Open Source Intelligence (OSINT): This type of intelligence is derived from publicly available sources, such as newspapers, books, radio broadcasts, or open databases. With the rise of the internet, OSINT has become increasingly important and voluminous, offering a wealth of data that can be legally collected and analyzed.

Geospatial Intelligence (GEOINT): GEOINT involves the exploitation and analysis of imagery and geospatial information to describe, assess, and visually depict physical features and geographically referenced activities on the Earth. GEOINT uses satellite images, maps, and even GPS data to paint a picture of terrain and movements.

Measurement & Signature Intelligence (MASINT): MASINT is a technical branch of intelligence gathering, which involves detecting, tracking, and identifying the unique signatures of fixed and dynamic target sources. This can include radar signatures, nuclear radiation analysis, and chemical composition analysis of various substances.

The efficacy of intelligence hinges on several core principles such as:

Accuracy: Intelligence must be as accurate as possible to provide reliable support for decision-makers.

Relevance: Information must be directly applicable to and actionable by the stakeholders involved.

Timeliness: Intelligence is often time-sensitive; timely intelligence can preempt threats and maximize strategic opportunities.

Usability: Data must be presented in a clear, concise manner that is immediately usable by decision-makers.

Security: Protecting intelligence sources and methods from potential adversaries is crucial to maintain the integrity and advantages of intelligence operations.

These foundational principles ensure that intelligence functions effectively as a tool for safeguarding national interests and enhancing strategic operations.

Intelligence analysis is the cornerstone of effective decision-making within any organization, particularly in military and defense operations. Let us further discuss how information is transformed into actionable intelligence through a structured process known as the intelligence cycle. Then we will further explore the key phases of this cycle, the various analytical techniques employed, and the challenges that analysts face in the quest to provide accurate and timely intelligence.

The intelligence cycle is a fundamental concept that describes the flow of information from collection to dissemination. It ensures that intelligence activities are continuously aligned with the operational needs of the organization. The cycle comprises several interrelated steps:

Step One, Collection: The process begins with the collection of information from a myriad of sources, which could include human sources (HUMINT), electronic intercepts (SIGINT), open-source materials (OSINT), and more. The effectiveness of the intelligence operation hinges on the breadth and depth of this collection phase.

Step Two, Processing: Once information is collected, it must be processed into a usable format. This might involve translation, decryption, or the formatting of data into databases. Processing makes the raw data accessible and ready for analysis.

Step Three, Analysis: Analysis is the heart of the intelligence cycle. Here, the processed information is critically examined and interpreted to produce actionable intelligence. Analysts apply various techniques to draw conclusions, identify trends, and forecast potential scenarios. This step transforms raw data into a coherent understanding of what the information signifies.

Step Four, Dissemination: The analyzed intelligence is then disseminated to policymakers, military commanders, or other relevant stakeholders who need this information to make informed decisions. The dissemination must be timely, and the intelligence presented in a manner that is clear and directly applicable to the needs of the users.

Step Five, Feedback: The final unofficial phase of the cycle is feedback, which involves the recipients of the intelligence providing input back to the analysts regarding the usefulness and relevance of the information received. Feedback is crucial for refining future intelligence efforts and ensuring that the intelligence cycle remains dynamic and responsive to the needs of its users.

To navigate through the vast quantities of data, intelligence analysts employ a range of techniques and tools. Here are some techniques used by analysts:

Link Analysis

Description: A method used to evaluate the relationships between nodes in a network, which can include individuals, organizations, and transactions. This technique is vital for mapping terrorist networks, criminal organizations, and social networks.

Tools: This could be software like Analyst's Notebook, Palantir, or network analysis modules in data science platforms like R and Python.

Skills: Analysts need to understand network theory, be proficient in using link analysis software, and have the ability to interpret complex network diagrams.

Pattern Analysis

Description: This involves statistical and computational techniques to detect regularities and anomalies in data sets, including time-series analysis for trend detection and clustering techniques to find hidden patterns.

Tools: Advanced analytics platforms like SAS, SPSS, or specialized software like Tableau for visual pattern recognition.

Skills: Strong statistical background, proficiency in analytical software, and the ability to synthesize information into actionable intelligence.

Geospatial Analysis

Description: The use of geographic data to create maps, integrate information, visualize scenarios, understand trends, and make decisions based on geographical data.

Tools: Geographic Information Systems (GIS) such as ArcGIS or QGIS and remote sensing software that can process satellite and aerial imagery.

Skills: Proficiency in GIS software, understanding of spatial statistics, and the ability to interpret satellite imagery and other geospatial data.

Data Mining and Big Data Analytics

Description: Techniques that extract patterns from large data sets by combining methods from statistics, artificial intelligence, and database management.

Tools: Big data platforms like Apache Hadoop, data mining tools like KNIME or RapidMiner, and database query languages like SQL.

Skills: Strong analytical skills, familiarity with big data technologies, proficiency in data mining algorithms, and the ability to handle and analyze very large data sets efficiently.

Challenges in Intelligence Analysis

Information Overload

Issue: Analysts often face the daunting task of sifting through massive amounts of data, which can result in critical information being overlooked due to sheer volume.

Mitigation Strategies: Employing data sorting and filtering techniques, and using machine learning algorithms to automate the identification of relevant data.

Bias and Subjectivity

Issue: Personal or institutional biases can color the analysis, leading to skewed or partial insights.

Mitigation Strategies: Implementing strict analytical protocols, regular training on cognitive biases, and fostering a culture of critical thinking and openness to challenge existing assumptions.

Technological Dependency

Issue: Over-reliance on technology can lead to vulnerabilities, especially if these systems are compromised, malfunction, or become obsolete.

Mitigation Strategies: Ensuring redundancy in analytical tools, continuous updating and patching of software, and maintaining a balance between automated and human-centric analysis processes.

Security and Secrecy

Issue: The need to protect sources and methods often conflicts with the requirement to share intelligence findings with relevant stakeholders.

Mitigation Strategies: Developing secure communication channels, employing robust encryption practices, and clear guidelines on information classification and declassification.

Dynamic Threats:

Cyber and Asymmetric Warfare

Issue: The fast-evolving nature of threats, particularly in cyber and asymmetric warfare, challenges existing intelligence frameworks which may not adapt quickly enough.

Mitigation Strategies: Continuous training in emerging threat vectors, fostering innovation in intelligence methods and tools, and agile intelligence practices that can pivot quickly in response to new information.

The process of intelligence analysis is critical to the success of civilian, military, and defense operations, providing key decision-makers with the insights needed to act effectively. By understanding and refining the intelligence cycle, employing robust analytical techniques, and overcoming the challenges inherent in intelligence work, organizations can enhance their strategic and operational capabilities. As the global security environment continues to evolve, so too must the techniques and tools of intelligence analysis to meet these new challenges head-on.

PART FOUR

Intelligence operations within State Defense Forces (SDFs) play a crucial role in supporting state-level security and response efforts. Let us examine the organizational structure of intelligence sections within SDFs and the specific roles played by Open Source Intelligence (OSINT) and Human Intelligence (HUMINT) in their operations.

In the U.S. Army, brigade-level units are supported by specialized staff sections, commonly referred to as "S Shops." These sections handle various operational, administrative, and logistical tasks essential to the unit's functioning. When adapted for State Defense Forces (SDFs), these S Shops serve similar roles but with modifications to meet specific state requirements and missions. Below is a breakdown of some of these sections, with a particular emphasis on S-2, the intelligence and information security section.

S-1

Role: Personnel

Manages all personnel-related activities, including administrative tasks, personnel support, and human resources services.

Responsible for the morale and welfare of troops, handling promotions, awards, and personnel readiness.

S-2

Role: Intelligence and Information Security

The S-2 section is crucial in gathering, analyzing, and securing intelligence relevant to SDF operations.

Responsible for the overall information security posture of the unit, ensuring sensitive information is protected against espionage and cyber threats.

Functions of S-2 in State Defense Forces

Intelligence Gathering: Collects OSINT, HUMINT, GEOINT, and other forms of intelligence pertinent to state security and SDF missions.

Threat Analysis: Analyzes potential threats to the state, including natural disasters, terrorism, cyber-attacks, and other emergencies.

Security Oversight: Implements and oversees measures to secure communications and information systems within the SDF.

Liaison Functions: Acts as the primary liaison with other state, local, and federal intelligence agencies to enhance collaboration and intelligence sharing.

Focus Areas

Cyber Intelligence: Due to the increasing threat of cyber-attacks, the S-2 section often emphasizes developing strong cyber intelligence and defense capabilities.

Disaster Intelligence: Focuses on gathering and analyzing information related to natural disasters or large public events, crucial for effective emergency management and response planning.

S-3

Role: Operations

Plans and coordinates all aspects of operations, training, and maneuvers.

Responsible for developing operational plans and directives for the deployment of troops during missions.

S-4

Role: Logistics

Manages supply chains and logistical support, including the procurement, distribution, maintenance, and replacement of equipment and supplies.

Ensures logistical readiness for all operations, including emergency responses.

S-5

Role: Planning

Although not always present in all units, the S-5 is typically responsible for long-term planning and civil-military operations.

Engages in strategic planning, coordination with civilian agencies, and public affairs.

S-6

Role: Communications

Oversees all aspects of military communications and information technology systems.

Ensures robust, secure, and reliable communications are maintained during all operations.

The S Shops provide essential support functions that enable State Defense Forces to operate effectively and efficiently. The S-2 section, in particular, plays a pivotal role by ensuring that intelligence and security operations are seamlessly integrated into the broader mission of the SDF. By focusing on areas like cyber intelligence and disaster intelligence, the S-2 helps prepare the SDF to respond to modern threats and challenges, safeguarding both the force and the community it serves. The adaptation of these functions to the needs and constraints of State Defense Forces is crucial for maintaining operational readiness and effectiveness.

The structure of intelligence sections in State Defense Forces is tailored to meet the specific needs and resources of each state. Generally, these positions within the scope of a military occupational specialty (MOS) are organized to ensure the effective collection, analysis, and dissemination of intelligence. Key skills & needs within the S2 typically include:

Intelligence Collection: Responsible for gathering information from various sources, this unit operates both OSINT and HUMINT operations, among other intelligence disciplines.

Analysis: Analysts in the S2 process and interpret the collected data to produce actionable intelligence. They work closely with S2 soldiers involved in collection to refine the focus of intelligence efforts based on their findings and the evolving needs of the SDF.

Dissemination: Soldiers in the S2 involved in dissemination ensure that intelligence products are promptly and securely delivered to the relevant decision-makers within the SDF and other state agencies as needed.

Command and Control: The leadership structure within the intelligence sections ensures coordination across units, maintaining oversight of operations and ensuring compliance with legal and ethical standards.

The effectiveness of an SDF's intelligence section is not solely dependent on its organizational structure but also on the integration of its operations with other state and national intelligence and law enforcement agencies.

Role of OSINT and HUMINT in State-Level Intelligence Gathering

Open-Source Intelligence (OSINT)

OSINT plays a vital role in the intelligence operations of State Defense Forces due to its accessibility and the breadth of information it offers. Key uses of OSINT include:

Disaster Response: OSINT can provide real-time information during natural disasters, such as flood levels from social media updates or damage assessments from news reports, which are crucial for timely and effective response.

Public Sentiment Analysis: Monitoring public sentiment on various issues can help SDFs and state governments understand and address public concerns more effectively, especially during crises or emergencies.

Event Monitoring: OSINT is used to monitor events that could impact public safety, including large public gatherings, protests, or state visits, allowing for better resource allocation and response planning.

Human Intelligence (HUMINT)

HUMINT, though more challenging to manage, offers critical insights that are not available through other means. Within SDFs, HUMINT may be employed in the following ways:

Community Engagement: SDF personnel often come from the communities they serve, providing them with unique access to local human sources. These connections can yield important information during crises or when assessing community needs and vulnerabilities.

Coordination with Local Authorities: SDFs work closely with local law enforcement and emergency services, allowing them to gather human intelligence through formal and informal partnerships.

Insider Threat Assessment: In situations involving security for state infrastructure or during large-scale events, HUMINT can be crucial for identifying and mitigating insider threats.

Challenges in OSINT and HUMINT Operations

While OSINT and HUMINT are invaluable for state-level intelligence, they come with challenges:

Verification: The abundance of information, especially from open sources, requires robust mechanisms to verify the accuracy and reliability of the data.

Privacy Concerns: HUMINT operations must be conducted with strict adherence to legal and ethical guidelines to protect the privacy and rights of individuals.

Resource Constraints: Effective training and management of HUMINT resources can be resource-intensive, posing challenges for SDFs operating with limited budgets.

The intelligence sections of State Defense Forces are crucial components in the state's overall security and emergency response framework. By effectively utilizing OSINT and HUMINT, along with other intelligence disciplines, SDFs can enhance their capability to respond to disasters, support civil authorities, and maintain state security. As threats evolve and new challenges emerge, the role of these intelligence operations will continue to expand, underscoring the need for ongoing investment in training, resources, and technology to support their mission.

Cyber and Geospatial Intelligence Capabilities in SDFs

As threats evolve in complexity and technical sophistication, State Defense Forces (SDFs) have adapted by enhancing their intelligence capabilities, particularly in the domains of cyber and geospatial intelligence (GEOINT). These capabilities are vital for protecting state assets, infrastructure, and citizens.

Cyber Intelligence in SDFs

Cyber intelligence involves the collection and analysis of information about potential and actual cyber threats. This is critical for State Defense Forces as cyber threats can impact critical infrastructure, disrupt state operations, and compromise sensitive data.

Cyber Surveillance and Monitoring: SDFs employ cyber intelligence teams to monitor state networks for signs of unauthorized access or other security threats. These teams use sophisticated software tools to detect anomalies that could indicate a cyber-attack.

Incident Response and Mitigation: In the event of a cyber incident, SDFs are equipped to respond promptly. They analyze the nature of the attack, identify the attackers (if possible), and mitigate damage by isolating affected systems and deploying protective measures.

Case Study:

Cyber Operations by the State Defense Force

A notable example involves the California State Guard's Cyber Network Defense Team. During a series of attempted cyber-attacks aimed at disrupting the state's essential services, the team used its cyber intelligence capabilities to identify and thwart malicious activities. They collaborated with local law enforcement and federal agencies, sharing intelligence that helped to pinpoint the source of the attacks and prevent further damage.

Geospatial Intelligence (GEOINT) in SDFs

GEOINT combines imagery, geographic information system (GIS) data, and satellite imagery to create a detailed understanding of physical features and activities on Earth, particularly those that impact state security and disaster response efforts.

Disaster Mapping and Analysis: SDFs utilize GEOINT to assess damage from natural disasters such as floods or earthquakes. Through satellite imagery and aerial reconnaissance, they can quickly ascertain the extent of damage, identify accessible routes for emergency responders, and determine the areas most in need of assistance.

Resource Allocation: By analyzing geospatial data, SDFs can optimize the deployment of resources. This is particularly useful in large-scale emergency situations where logistics and timely response are crucial.

Case Study:

GEOINT Application in Disaster Response

An example of successful GEOINT application occurred during the flooding in Louisiana. The Louisiana State Guard used GEOINT to map the affected areas, integrating data from various sources, including satellite images and field reports. This comprehensive geospatial analysis enabled them to efficiently coordinate rescue operations and manage evacuation plans, significantly reducing potential casualties and accelerating recovery efforts.

The cyber and geospatial intelligence capabilities of State Defense Forces represent crucial components of their overall intelligence operations. These capabilities not only enhance the state's defensive measures against cyber threats but also improve their responsiveness to natural disasters and other crises through accurate and timely intelligence. As technological advancements continue, the role of cyber and GEOINT in SDFs is expected to grow, further integrating these modern intelligence disciplines into their standard operational frameworks. This progression underscores the need for continuous investment in training, technology, and collaboration at all levels of government to maintain and enhance these critical capabilities.

PART FIVE

Effective intelligence operations within State Defense Forces (SDFs) are pivotal not only for security but also for supporting a wide range of state government functions. This part explores how the strategic use of intelligence can enhance state emergency management and foster collaborative efforts with the National Guard and other military components, ensuring a unified response to both crises and routine state functions.

Integration of Intelligence with State Emergency Management

Best Practices

Comprehensive Risk Assessments: Utilizing intelligence to conduct detailed risk assessments allows SDFs to identify potential vulnerabilities within the state, from natural disasters to cybersecurity threats. This proactive approach enables tailored contingency planning.

Real time Information Sharing: Establishing protocols for real-time intelligence sharing during emergencies ensures that all involved agencies have access to the same information, facilitating a coordinated response. For example, during a natural disaster, real-time GEOINT and OSINT can provide updates on affected areas, helping to optimize rescue and relief efforts.

Regular Training and Simulations: Conducting regular training exercises based on intelligence scenarios helps prepare emergency management teams and SDF personnel to respond effectively. These simulations should incorporate realistic scenarios based on historical data and predictive intelligence analyses.

Strategic Applications

Pre-Event Planning: Intelligence can inform the planning and allocation of resources before an emergency strikes, such as pre-positioning supplies in areas likely to be affected by natural disasters.

During-Event Coordination: Intelligence operations can provide command centers with ongoing situational updates that are crucial for dynamic decision-making during an emergency.

Post-Event Analysis: After an emergency, intelligence can help in the assessment of response effectiveness, identifying successful strategies and areas needing improvement, which is essential for refining future emergency responses.

Collaborative Intelligence Sharing with the National Guard and Other Military Components

Best Practices

Establishing Joint Intelligence Centers: One effective practice is the establishment of joint intelligence centers where SDFs, the National Guard, and other military components can share insights and data. These centers act as hubs for intelligence fusion and operational coordination.

Standardized Communication Protocols: Developing and maintaining standardized communication protocols ensures that intelligence sharing is swift and effective, minimizing the risk of miscommunication during joint operations.

Cross-Training Programs & Joint Excersizes: Implementing cross-training programs can enhance mutual understanding of capabilities and procedures, thereby improving the integration of intelligence operations across different military components.

Strategic Applications

Unified Threat Assessments: Collaborative intelligence efforts lead to more comprehensive threat assessments, combining data from various sources for a more complete security picture. This unified approach is crucial in addressing complex threats that may span multiple jurisdictions.

Enhance Situational Awareness: Sharing intelligence

among SDFs, the National Guard, and other components enhances situational awareness at all levels of command. This collective awareness is vital for effective operational planning and execution.

Resource Optimization: By sharing intelligence, state military components can optimize the use of resources, avoiding duplication of efforts and ensuring that the most accurate and comprehensive intelligence guides deployments and operations.

The strategic use of intelligence by State Defense Forces significantly enhances their ability to support state government functions, particularly in areas of emergency management and collaboration with other military entities. Best practices in intelligence integration and sharing not only improve the effectiveness of response efforts but also strengthen the state's overall security and resilience. As challenges evolve, so too must the strategies and technologies employed in intelligence operations, ensuring that SDFs remain capable and prepared to meet future demands.

As we conclude our exploration of the role of intelligence within State Defense Forces (SDFs), it is important to recapitulate the key insights gained and to contemplate the future trajectory of these forces in the ever-evolving security landscape. This final part summarizes the critical roles and capabilities of SDF intelligence, identifies future challenges and opportunities, and offers recommendations for enhancing their effectiveness.

State Defense Forces play a vital role in supplementing national defense and enhancing state-level emergency response capabilities through focused intelligence operations.

Key points include

Diverse Intelligence Disciplines: SDFs utilize a variety of intelligence types, including OSINT, HUMINT, SIGINT, and GEOINT, to gather comprehensive situational awareness that supports state and local authorities.

Support to Civil Operations: Intelligence operations within SDFs significantly bolster state emergency management by providing crucial information that guides disaster response and mitigation efforts.

Collaboration and Integration: SDFs actively collaborate with the National Guard and other military components, sharing intelligence that enhances operational effectiveness and strategic decision-making across multiple echelons of command.

Adaptability and Specialization: SDF intelligence units are highly adaptable, capable of tailoring their operations to meet the specific needs and challenges faced by their respective states.

Future Challenges and Opportunities for SDFs
Looking ahead

SDFs face several challenges that also present unique opportunities for growth and enhancement. let us look at some of these challenges.

Technological Advancements: Rapid advancements in technology, particularly in cyber operations and artificial intelligence, offer both challenges in keeping pace with potential threats and opportunities to enhance intelligence capabilities.

Resource Constraints: While funding and resources are perennial challenges for SDFs, these limitations also drive innovation in maximizing efficiency and effectiveness through creative solutions and partnerships.

Interagency Coordination: As threats become more complex and multifaceted, enhancing coordination and cooperation not just within military branches, but also with civilian agencies and private sector partners, will be crucial.

Legal and Ethical Considerations: The expanding role of intelligence operations necessitates continuous evaluation of legal frameworks and ethical guidelines to ensure that the rights and privacy of citizens are protected.

To navigate future challenges and maximize the potential of SDFs, several recommendations are proposed

Enhanced Training Programs: Develop comprehensive training programs that include advanced intelligence analysis techniques, cyber security measures, and the use of emerging technologies.

Investment in Technology: Prioritize investments in new technologies that can enhance intelligence gathering and analysis capabilities, such as AI-driven analytics platforms and more sophisticated communication and encryption tools.

Strengthen Legal Frameworks: Review and strengthen legal and regulatory frameworks to ensure they keep pace with technological advancements and adequately address new forms of threats.

Foster Public-Private Partnerships: Encourage partnerships with academic institutions and the private sector to leverage external expertise, technology, and resources.

Expand Community Engagement: Increase engagement with local communities to foster a broader understanding of the SDF's role and capabilities, which can enhance public trust and cooperation during state emergencies.

The intelligence capabilities of State Defense Forces are integral to their mission of supporting state and national security. As these forces continue to adapt to new challenges, their success will increasingly depend on strategic foresight, interagency collaboration, and a commitment to continuous improvement and adaptation. Looking forward, the evolution of SDF intelligence operations will play a pivotal role in shaping a resilient and responsive state defense framework, ready to meet the complexities of tomorrow's security environment.

ADDENDUM INTRODUCTION

Thank you for engaging with the content of this book. If you feel that your journey through the landscape of State Military Intelligence has concluded, you may consider this the endpoint. However, for those eager to delve further into the intricate world of intelligence analysis, the subsequent sections of this book offer a comprehensive exploration.

This addendum is designed to enrich your understanding by providing an in-depth examination of various intelligence tools and methodologies, including a detailed look at Signals Intelligence (SIGINT) and Open Source Intelligence (OSINT). Our aim is to enhance your grasp of the operational and strategic elements that define intelligence work within the broader United States intelligence community.

Whether you're a professional in the field, a student of intelligence studies, or simply a curious reader, these additional insights will equip you with a deeper knowledge of the critical tools and processes that underpin effective intelligence operations.

Proceed if you wish to expand your understanding of these dynamic and pivotal aspects of intelligence work.

ADDENDUM PART I

Understanding the Intelligence Cycle

The intelligence cycle is a structured process used by various intelligence agencies and organizations to guide the stages of intelligence gathering, processing, analysis, and dissemination. It is the fundamental framework through which intelligence operations are conducted, ensuring that information is collected systematically and analyzed thoroughly before it informs decision-making. This part explores each stage of the intelligence cycle, providing a deep dive into the mechanisms that underpin successful intelligence operations.

Planning and Direction

The first stage of the intelligence cycle involves setting objectives and deciding what information needs to be collected to support decision-makers. This stage is critical as it sets the agenda for the entire intelligence operation.

Key Activities:

 - Identifying intelligence requirements based on the needs of policymakers or military leaders.

 - Prioritizing tasks to efficiently allocate resources.

- Developing specific questions that intelligence collection will aim to answer.

Effective planning ensures that the intelligence community focuses its efforts on gathering relevant and actionable information, thus optimizing the resources and directing efforts strategically.

Collection

Collection is the second stage in the cycle. Collection is the gathering of raw data from various sources that may hold information relevant to intelligence needs. This stage uses diverse methods and sources, including human sources (HUMINT), electronic signals (SIGINT), imagery (IMINT), and open sources (OSINT).

Key Activities:

- Deploying assets to gather needed information, whether through covert operations, communications interception, satellite imagery, or public media.

- Ensuring the reliability and legality of the collection methods.

- Managing and coordinating multiple collection efforts to cover all necessary aspects of the intelligence requirement.

The collection phase is where the theoretical needs defined in the planning stage begin to materialize as concrete data, which forms the foundation for all subsequent analysis.

Processing

Once information is collected, it needs to be converted into a format that can be easily analyzed. This includes translation, decryption, and the formatting of data into intelligible forms. Thus processing is the third stage of the cycle.

Key Activities:

- Transcribing intercepted communications.

- Decrypting coded messages.

- Sorting and prioritizing data for further analysis.

Processing ensures that the raw data is in a usable state for analysts to begin their work. Incomplete or improperly processed data can lead to inaccuracies in the analysis phase.

Analysis

Analysis is the fourth stage and the core of the intelligence cycle, this is where raw information is transformed into intelligence. Analysts evaluate the data for its relevance, reliability, and significance, integrating it with existing knowledge to draw conclusions and develop assessments.

Key Activities:

- Identifying patterns, trends, and anomalies.

- Employing analytical techniques such as link analysis, geospatial analysis, and predictive analytics.

- Preparing intelligence reports that synthesize findings in a clear and actionable manner.

This phase is crucial for producing intelligence that is not only informative but also actionable. Good analysis informs strategic decisions, policy formulation, and operational planning.

Dissemination

The final stage of the intelligence cycle is the dissemination of intelligence products to the end users, typically decision-makers who will use the information to inform policies, strategies, and operations.

Key Activities:

- Distributing intelligence reports to relevant stakeholders.

- Presenting findings in briefings and supporting decision-makers in understanding the implications.

- Ensuring the security and appropriate classification level of the disseminated intelligence.

Effective dissemination ensures that the intelligence reaches the right people at the right time and in the right format, thereby enabling informed decision-making.

The intelligence cycle is a dynamic and continuous process that requires meticulous attention to detail at every stage to ensure the production of high-quality intelligence. By understanding each phase of the cycle, intelligence professionals can better tailor their approaches to meet the complex demands of national security, defense, and strategic policy-making. This cyclical process not only supports current operational needs but also prepares the intelligence apparatus to adapt and respond to emerging threats and challenges.

ADDENDUM PART II

Behavior Detection and Analysis

Behavior detection and analysis is a critical discipline within the fields of security and intelligence. It involves the systematic observation and interpretation of human behaviors to identify potential security threats, deception, or irregular activities. This part explores the foundational concepts, methodologies, and practical applications of behavior detection and analysis, particularly in the context of enhancing security measures and intelligence gathering.

Understanding Behavior Detection and Analysis

Behavior detection and analysis refers to the techniques used to assess human actions and intentions based on observable behaviors and non-verbal cues. It is commonly employed in environments where security is a priority, such as airports, border crossings, and public events.
The primary purpose of behavior detection is to proactively identify individuals who may pose a threat before they can act. By analyzing patterns of behavior that deviate from the norm, security personnel can intervene early, potentially preventing criminal activities or terrorist attacks.

Key Concepts in Behavior Detection

Baseline Behavior: Establishing a baseline involves observing the typical behavior of individuals in a specific environment to understand what is considered normal. Any deviation from this baseline may indicate stress, fear, deception, or malicious intent.

Stress, fear, and Deception Indicators: These are specific behaviors that may signify psychological stress or attempts to deceive. Common indicators include excessive sweating, avoiding eye contact, fidgeting, and inconsistencies in verbal explanations.

Micro-expressions: Brief, involuntary facial expressions that reveal true emotions. Trained analysts use these fleeting signs to detect underlying feelings that an individual may attempt to conceal.

Methodologies Employed in Behavior Detection

Direct Observation: Analysts are trained to observe people directly, noting any behaviors that stand out from established baselines. This can be done via surveillance cameras or through in-person monitoring.

Analytical Techniques: Techniques such as the Facial Action Coding System (FACS) are used to decode facial expressions and body language. Analysts also employ behavior analysis tools to interpret the psychological significance of observed behaviors.

Interrogation and Interaction: Engaging potentially suspicious individuals in conversation can reveal additional behavioral cues. Questions designed to elicit stress or deception can be particularly revealing.

Best Practices in Behavior Detection and Analysis

Continuous Training: Ongoing training is crucial for behavior detection personnel to stay current with the latest techniques and technologies. Regular drills and workshops help refine observation and analysis skills.

Multi-Layered Approach: Integrating behavior detection with other security measures, such as biometric screening and electronic surveillance, creates a robust security infrastructure that can adapt to diverse threats.

Ethical Considerations: It's essential to balance security needs with respect for individual privacy and rights. Behavior detection programs must operate within legal frameworks and respect cultural differences.

Data-Driven Enhancements: Incorporating data analytics and machine learning can improve the accuracy of behavior detection systems. Analyzing large datasets can help refine indicators of suspicious behavior and enhance predictive capabilities.

Applications in Security and Intelligence

Behavior detection is employed in various high-risk settings to preemptively identify threats. It is particularly effective in crowded public spaces like airports, train stations, and large events. Intelligence agencies also use behavior detection techniques during interrogations and surveillance operations to assess the credibility of information and the intent of individuals.

Behavior detection and analysis is a dynamic field that plays a vital role in modern security and intelligence operations. As threats continue to evolve, so too must the methodologies and technologies used to detect and analyze behavior. By understanding the subtleties of human behavior and applying this knowledge judiciously, security professionals can significantly enhance their ability to preempt and mitigate potential threats.

ADDENDUM PART III

Signals Intelligence (SIGINT)

Signals Intelligence (SIGINT) is a crucial branch of intelligence that involves the interception, collection, and analysis of electronic signals to gather information. This part explores the foundational aspects of SIGINT, its methodologies, the challenges it faces, and its significance in national security and intelligence operations.

Understanding Signals Intelligence

SIGINT encompasses the interception and analysis of electronic communications and signals emitted by communications equipment, radars, and other electronic systems. It is divided into two main subcategories:

Communications Intelligence (COMINT): Involves the interception and analysis of voice and data communications between people, including phone calls, emails, and instant messages.

Electronic Intelligence (ELINT): Focuses on the interception and analysis of non-communicative electronic signals, primarily from radar and other electronic systems.

The primary purpose of SIGINT is to support military

and strategic decision-making by providing insights into the capabilities, actions, and intentions of adversaries. It is crucial for both national defense and offensive strategic operations.

Methodologies Employed in SIGINT

Collection:

Signal Capture: Using various technologies and devices to intercept electronic communications and signals. This includes satellite dishes, radio receivers, and specialized interception equipment deployed on aircraft, ships, and ground stations.

Signal Processing: Transforming raw electronic signals into a format that can be analyzed, involving signal demodulation, decoding, and decryption.

Analysis:

Content Analysis: Examining the content of intercepted communications to extract valuable intelligence, such as plans, strategies, and operational details.

Traffic Analysis: Studying the external characteristics of communications, such as sender, receiver, frequency, and timing, to identify communication patterns and networks.

Dissemination: Providing processed intelligence to decision-makers in an actionable form, often as part of broader intelligence reports or briefings.

Challenges in SIGINT

Volume and Complexity: The sheer volume and complexity of global communications pose significant challenges in filtering and analyzing relevant information without becoming overwhelmed.

Encryption and Security Measures: Advances in encryption technologies and security protocols make it increasingly difficult to intercept and decipher communications.

Legal and Ethical Considerations: SIGINT operations often raise privacy concerns and legal issues, particularly regarding the interception of communications without consent. Ensuring operations comply with domestic and international laws is crucial.

Technological Advancements: Keeping pace with rapid technological advancements in communications is essential to maintain effective SIGINT capabilities.

Best Practices in SIGINT Operations

Legal Compliance: Ensuring all SIGINT activities are authorized by law and conducted with the necessary warrants or permissions to mitigate legal risks and protect civil liberties.

Minimization Procedures: Implementing strict data minimization procedures to protect the privacy of non-targeted individuals inadvertently caught in SIGINT operations.

Advanced Analytics: Utilizing advanced data analytics and artificial intelligence to manage large datasets more effectively and identify relevant intelligence faster.

Collaboration and Sharing: Enhancing collaboration between different intelligence agencies and allied nations to share SIGINT resources and insights, thereby improving the overall effectiveness of intelligence efforts.

Signals Intelligence remains one of the most potent forms of intelligence gathering available to national security agencies. As the digital landscape evolves, so too does the field of SIGINT, continuously adapting to new technologies and challenges. By effectively leveraging SIGINT capabilities, nations can protect their interests and maintain strategic advantages over potential adversaries, ensuring national security in an increasingly complex global environment.

ADDENDUM PART IV

Human Intelligence (HUMINT)

Human Intelligence (HUMINT) involves the collection of information from human sources. As one of the oldest forms of intelligence gathering, HUMINT plays a crucial role in the broader intelligence apparatus, providing insights that are often unattainable through other intelligence disciplines. This part delves into the nuances of HUMINT, its methods, the challenges it faces, and its critical role in security and intelligence operations.

Understanding Human Intelligence

HUMINT is the collection of intelligence through interpersonal contact. Unlike SIGINT or IMINT (Imagery Intelligence), HUMINT is derived directly from human sources or "human assets." This can include diplomatic sources, espionage, interrogations, and liaison operations or from publicly available information such as interviews and first-hand observations.

The primary purpose of HUMINT is to gather information about the intentions, compositions, capabilities, and environments of adversaries or potential adversaries. It is particularly valuable for understanding nuanced political and cultural contexts that are inaccessible to technical means of intelligence collection.

Methodologies Employed in HUMINT

Espionage: Involves undercover agents and spies collecting sensitive or classified information from within a foreign nation or organization.

Debriefings: Gathering intelligence from people who have had access to valuable information, such as defectors, refugees, travelers, and released prisoners of war.

Interrogations: Systematically questioning cooperative or captured personnel to extract valuable intelligence.

Liaison Operations: Collaborating with foreign security services to gather intelligence that serves mutual interests.

Covert and Overt Collection: Using both covert (hidden from the subject) and overt (open and possibly known to the subject) methods to gather information from willing or unwitting sources.

Challenges in HUMINT

Operational Risks: HUMINT operations often involve significant personal risks to the agents involved, especially in hostile regions or when handling sensitive information.

Counterintelligence Threats: Adversaries actively work to deceive, detect, and neutralize HUMINT operations, requiring continuous efforts to secure operations and protect sources.

Reliability of Information: The accuracy of information gathered from human sources can be variable. Information may be intentionally misleading or simply inaccurate, necessitating rigorous verification.

Ethical and Legal Issues: HUMINT operations can raise ethical concerns, particularly with regards to espionage and interrogations. Ensuring that operations comply with international law and ethical standards is crucial.

Best Practices in HUMINT Operations

Rigorous Training and Preparation: Agents should receive extensive training in communication skills, cultural awareness, operational security, and stress management to operate effectively and ethically.

Source and Information Validation: Employing multiple methods to confirm the reliability of the information provided by human sources, including cross-referencing with other intelligence inputs.

Use of Technology: Integrating technology to manage and secure operations, such as encrypted communications and advanced surveillance techniques to monitor meetings and movements safely.

Strong Legal Framework: Developing and adhering to a strong legal framework to guide HUMINT activities, ensuring they respect human rights and international norms.

Human Intelligence remains a fundamentally important aspect of the intelligence collection spectrum. Its direct human element allows for a depth and subtlety of understanding that complements other intelligence disciplines. As the global environment becomes increasingly complex, the ability to effectively manage and utilize HUMINT will continue to be a strategic asset, providing crucial insights that inform and enhance national security strategies.

ADDENDUM PART V

Open Source Intelligence (OSINT)

Open Source Intelligence (OSINT) refers to the process of collecting and analyzing information from publicly available sources for intelligence purposes. In the digital age, where vast amounts of data are accessible via the internet, OSINT has become an increasingly critical component of the intelligence community's toolkit. This part explores the definition, methodologies, challenges, and strategic importance of OSINT in modern intelligence operations.

Understanding Open Source Intelligence

OSINT encompasses any information that can legally be gathered from free, publicly available sources. This includes a wide range of printed materials, television, radio broadcasts, the internet, and more recently, social media platforms and open government databases. The key is that the information is accessible to the public and does not require any type of clandestine methods to obtain.

The primary purpose of OSINT is to collect valuable information that is openly available but scattered across various sources. It supports a wide array of intelligence needs, including situational awareness, threat assessment, and decision-making support across both governmental and non-governmental sectors.

Methodologies Employed in OSINT

Data Collection:

Internet Research: Utilizing search engines, websites, and digital archives to gather information.

Social Media Monitoring: Analyzing content from platforms like Twitter, Facebook, and Instagram to gather real-time data on public opinion, trends, and significant events.

Public Records: Accessing government documents, official reports, registries, and other public sector data that are openly available.

Data Analysis:

Sentiment Analysis: Using natural language processing tools to analyze public sentiment and emotional tones within large volumes of text.

Trend Analysis: Identifying patterns or trends in public data that could indicate emerging threats or opportunities.

Geospatial Analysis: Employing mapping software and location data to assess geographic patterns and relationships.

Challenges in OSINT

Information Overload: The vast quantity of available information can be overwhelming, making it difficult to identify what is relevant and accurate.

Verification Issues: The open nature of the sources often means that the reliability and accuracy of the information can vary significantly. Verifying facts is crucial and can be time-consuming.

Rapidly Changing Information: The dynamic nature of open sources, especially online and social media, means that information can change quickly, requiring constant updates.
Legal and Ethical Considerations: While OSINT utilizes publicly available information, there are still legal and ethical considerations regarding privacy, especially with information gleaned from social media platforms.

Best Practices in OSINT Operations

Advanced Analytical Tools: Implementing sophisticated software and analytical tools that can automate the collection and initial analysis of large datasets to manage information overload effectively.

Continuous Training: Keeping analysts trained in the latest technologies and methodologies is crucial as digital landscapes and tools evolve rapidly.

Multi-source Corroboration: Ensuring that information is corroborated through multiple sources or other intelligence methods before it is used in decision-making processes.

Ethical Guidelines: Establishing clear guidelines for what constitutes ethical OSINT practices, particularly in respect to privacy concerns and data protection laws.

Open Source Intelligence is an indispensable part of the intelligence framework, providing a wealth of information that is both cost-effective and broadly accessible. As technology evolves and the volume of publicly available information continues to expand, OSINT will play an increasingly vital role in shaping the intelligence landscape. By leveraging advanced technologies and maintaining rigorous standards for data collection and analysis, intelligence agencies can harness the power of OSINT to enhance their operational capabilities and strategic insights.

ADDENDUM PART VI

Geospatial Intelligence (GEOINT)

Geospatial Intelligence (GEOINT) involves the exploitation and analysis of imagery and geospatial information to describe, assess, and visually depict physical features and geographically referenced activities on the Earth. GEOINT encompasses a wide range of data sources, including satellite imagery, geographic information systems (GIS), and aerial photography. This part will explore the fundamentals of GEOINT, its methodologies, applications, and the strategic value it adds to military operations, disaster response, and national security.

Understanding Geospatial Intelligence

GEOINT goes beyond the simple taking of pictures; it integrates multiple sources of geospatial data and information, including maps, GPS data, satellite imagery, and other large sets of geographic data. This intelligence discipline is vital for making strategic decisions in both military and civilian sectors due to its ability to provide a time-sensitive, three-dimensional view of a particular geographical area.

The primary purpose of GEOINT is to help decision-makers visualize and understand the physical layout and geographical context of operational environments. It plays a crucial role in disaster management, urban planning, environmental monitoring, and security and intelligence operations.

Methodologies Employed in GEOINT

Data Collection:

Satellite Imagery: Using satellites to capture images of the Earth, which can reveal valuable information about terrain, infrastructure, and environmental conditions.

Aerial Photography: Employing aircraft and drones to take detailed photographs from the air, often used for mapping and tactical analysis.

GIS Data Analysis: Integrating various data forms and sources into a GIS to analyze spatial relationships and patterns.

Data Analysis:

Image Processing: Techniques such as stitching, enhancing, and analyzing images to derive useful intelligence.

Feature Recognition: Identifying and classifying natural and man-made features in the imagery.

Change Detection: Monitoring changes over time in geographic areas to detect significant alterations or ongoing trends.

Challenges in GEOINT

Data Volume and Management: The sheer amount of geospatial data collected from various sensors can be overwhelming and requires robust data management systems to store, process, and retrieve.

Rapid Technological Changes: Keeping up with rapid advancements in technology and satellite capabilities can be challenging, necessitating ongoing training and technical upgrades.

Accuracy and Resolution Constraints: Limitations in the resolution of images, which can affect the accuracy and usability of the intelligence gathered.

Privacy and Legal Concerns: Navigating legal restrictions related to surveillance and privacy when using geospatial data, especially data captured over sovereign territories or in densely populated areas.

Best Practices in GEOINT Operations

Integration with Other Intel Disciplines: Combining GEOINT with HUMINT, SIGINT, and other intelligence disciplines to provide a more comprehensive understanding of the operational environment.

Advanced Analytical Techniques: Leveraging machine

learning and artificial intelligence to enhance image analysis and feature recognition capabilities.

Collaborative Partnerships: Engaging in partnerships with other nations, private sector entities, and academic institutions to enhance technological capabilities and data sharing.

Ethical and Legal Compliance: Ensuring all GEOINT operations are conducted within the bounds of national and international law, including adhering to privacy laws and regulations.

Geospatial Intelligence is a critical component of modern intelligence and security operations, offering unique insights that are not available through other intelligence disciplines. Its ability to provide detailed visual and spatial data makes it indispensable for planning and operational decision-making across a wide range of applications. As satellite and imaging technologies continue to evolve, so too will the capabilities and strategic value of GEOINT, solidifying its role as a key pillar of national security infrastructure.

ADDENDUM PART VI

Measurement and Signature Intelligence (MASINT)

Measurement and Signature Intelligence (MASINT) is a technically complex field of intelligence gathering, which involves the detection, classification, and identification of unique signatures emitted by sources such as radar systems, nuclear weapons, and chemical substances. This part will delve into the essentials of MASINT, exploring its methodologies, the types of data it collects, its applications, and the unique challenges it faces.

Understanding Measurement and Signature Intelligence

MASINT is distinguished from other intelligence disciplines by its reliance on quantitative and qualitative analysis of physical attributes to gather actionable intelligence. Unlike SIGINT that focuses on the interception of signals, or GEOINT that interprets visual imagery, MASINT analyzes the physical phenomena, such as spectral, thermal, or seismic data emitted by sources to provide detailed insights into their characteristics and capabilities.

The primary purpose of MASINT is to track, identify, and characterize specific events, facilities, or equipment through the physical signatures they produce. This intelligence is crucial for verification of arms control agreements, assessment of military capabilities, and detection of emerging threats.

Methodologies Employed in MASINT

Data Collection:

Spectral Analysis: Uses sensors to measure the electromagnetic spectrum, identifying unique chemical signatures from industrial or military processes.

Radar Analysis: Detects and characterizes objects by analyzing the radar signals they reflect, differentiating between types of aircraft, missiles, or ships.

Seismic Analysis: Monitors seismic activities to distinguish between natural earthquakes and underground explosions or other man-made seismic events.

Data Analysis:

Pattern Recognition: Identifying distinctive patterns in the collected data that indicate specific types of activities or operational behaviors.

Anomaly Detection: Spotting deviations from normal patterns that may indicate covert operations or emerging threats.

Data Fusion: Integrating MASINT data with information from other intelligence sources to enhance the reliability and accuracy of the findings.

Challenges in MASINT

Technological Complexity: MASINT operations require sophisticated, often bespoke, sensor technologies and data processing systems, making it a resource-intensive intelligence discipline.

High Specialization: The analysis of MASINT data typically requires highly specialized knowledge in fields such as physics, chemistry, and geoscience, necessitating a dedicated pool of expert analysts.

Data Overload: The vast amounts of raw data produced by MASINT sensors can overwhelm analysis processes, requiring effective filtering and prioritization systems.

Environmental Interference: Natural phenomena such as weather or geological variations can interfere with the detection and accuracy of MASINT readings, complicating the analysis.

Best Practices in MASINT Operations

Continuous Technology Upgrades: Regularly updating sensor technologies and analytical tools to keep pace with advancements in the fields relevant to MASINT.

Interdisciplinary Training: Providing analysts with interdisciplinary training to enhance their ability to interpret complex MASINT data across different scientific domains.

Collaboration with Scientific Community: Engaging with the academic and scientific communities to incorporate the latest research findings and technological innovations into MASINT practices.

Robust Validation Mechanisms: Implementing robust mechanisms for validating and corroborating MASINT data to ensure the accuracy and reliability of intelligence products.

Measurement and Signature Intelligence is a vital component of the modern intelligence apparatus, capable of providing unique insights that are not obtainable through other means. Its applications range from monitoring compliance with international treaties to detecting hidden military activities and emerging threats. As threats become more sophisticated and varied, the strategic importance of MASINT is likely to increase, underscoring the need for continued investment in this technologically advanced field.

LETTER TO THE READER

Dear Reader,

First and foremost, I wish to express my profound gratitude for your decision to engage in this work. This book is not merely a collection of pages but a synthesis of my professional reflections on the complex world of state military intelligence. This book was written in a way to allow someone with no background in intelligence to pick up this book and read it in simple and easy to understand terminology and layout. Your interaction with this content completes a meaningful circuit, connecting my insights with your curiosity and understanding. For this, I am deeply thankful.

I firmly believe in the free flow of ideas and knowledge. It is through the sharing of our experiences, insights, and understanding that we foster broader comprehension, inspire positive change, and contribute to a richer, more informed society. In this spirit, I invite you to utilize the knowledge and perspectives offered in this book. Whether they inspire you, provide clarity, or serve as a foundation for your own ventures in writing or research, please feel free to reference and build upon this work. I ask only that you attribute any direct citations or adaptations to this original effort. This small act maintains our connection as author and reader and honors the age-old tradition of storytelling and scholarly discourse that binds us.

The thought that my writing might ignite a new idea, offer a fresh perspective, or even provide reassurance is both humbling and rewarding. Literature, especially non-fiction that delves into the realms of military and intelligence, is a powerful dialogue that transcends boundaries of space and time, a dialogue that rightfully belongs to us all. If my contributions can enrich this ongoing conversation, I consider it a great privilege and honor.

As you move forward, whether you absorb these insights quietly or integrate them into your broader academic or professional projects, know that you have my full support and blessing. It is my sincere hope that the discussions and data presented here, born from meticulous study and real-world application, will inspire and inform your endeavors. May this book serve as a bridge connecting the theoretical to the practical, enhancing both our understanding of state military intelligence and its crucial role in our security landscape.

Thank you once again for joining me on this intellectual journey. Here's to the continued growth, learning, and exploration that await us both.

With sincere appreciation and warmest regards,

The Honorable Daniel Bowen

Commonwealth of Kentucky, Colonel
32nd Degree, Master Mason

GLOSSARY OF KEY TERMS

Artificial Intelligence (AI): Technology that enables computers to perform tasks that normally require human intelligence, such as recognizing speech, making decisions, and translating languages. In the context of intelligence operations, AI can process large datasets quickly to identify patterns and anomalies.

Civil-Military Operations: Activities of the military that involve the management of relationships between military forces, governmental and non-governmental civilian organizations and authorities, and the civilian populace. These operations help facilitate military operations and consolidate operational objectives.

Cyber Intelligence: The collection, processing, analysis, and dissemination of information from cyberspace that is used to understand threats to internal and external security. It includes monitoring potential cyber-attacks and safeguarding information systems.

Disaster Response: Organized, strategic procedures that are enacted in response to a natural or man-made disaster. The goal is to provide immediate assistance to maintain life, improve health, and support the morale of the affected population.

Geospatial Intelligence (GEOINT): Intelligence about the human activity on earth derived from the exploitation and analysis of imagery and geospatial information that describes, assesses, and visually depicts physical features and geographically referenced activities.

Human Intelligence (HUMINT): Intelligence gathered from human sources. This can include espionage where trained agents gather covert information, or the debriefing of refugees, defectors, and prisoners of war.

Intelligence Cycle: The process by which information is collected, analyzed, and made into intelligence and then disseminated to the appropriate leaders. This cycle includes direction, collection, processing, analysis, dissemination, and feedback.

Measurement and Signature Intelligence (MASINT): A technical branch of intelligence gathering which involves detecting, tracking, and identifying the distinctive signatures of fixed and dynamic target sources like radar signatures or nuclear radiation.

Militia: An armed force composed of ordinary citizens to provide defense, emergency law enforcement, or paramilitary service, in times of emergency without being paid a full-time salary or committed to a fixed term of service.

Open Source Intelligence (OSINT): Intelligence derived from publicly available sources such as newspapers, books, radio broadcasts, or open databases. With the rise of the internet, OSINT has become increasingly important and voluminous, offering a wealth of data that can be legally collected and analyzed.

Posse Comitatus Act: A U.S. federal law (18 U.S.C. § 1385) intended to limit the powers of the federal government in using federal military personnel to enforce domestic policies. It acts to prevent the direct participation of federal military forces in domestic law enforcement activities unless expressly authorized by law.

Signals Intelligence (SIGINT): Intelligence-gathering by interception of signals, whether communications between people (communications intelligence—abbreviated to COMINT) or from electronic signals not directly used in communication (electronic intelligence—abbreviated to ELINT).

State Defense Forces (SDFs): Military units that operate under the sole authority of a state government; SDFs are not regulated by the National Guard Bureau nor are they funded by the federal government. SDFs' duties include emergency and disaster response, search and rescue, counter-drug operations, and augmentation of National Guard or other military operations as required.

Title 10 and Title 32 of the United States Code: Legal federal codes that outline the role of the federal armed forces and the federal and state militia. Title 10 governs the U.S. Armed Forces, while Title 32 pertains to the National Guard and State Defense Force role under state and federal law.

Unmanned Aerial Systems (Drones): Aircraft without a human pilot aboard, controlled from an operator on the ground. In intelligence operations, drones are used for surveillance, gathering imagery intelligence, and sometimes for delivery of payloads.

Algorithmic Decision-Making: The process of making decisions based on pre-set algorithms and computational processes, often used in analyzing large datasets within intelligence operations to predict patterns and behaviors.

Asymmetric Warfare: Conflict between parties of unequal strength, where the weaker party uses non-traditional and often unexpected tactics against the stronger opponent, such as guerrilla warfare or cyber attacks.

Command and Control (C&C): The exercise of authority and direction by a properly designated commander over assigned and attached forces in the accomplishment of a mission. It involves the management of personnel and resources.

Data Mining: The process of analyzing large datasets to discover patterns and relationships that can inform decision-making. In intelligence operations, data mining is crucial for extracting valuable insights from vast amounts of information.

Debriefing: The process of questioning returnees, defectors, or individuals with valuable information to extract intelligence or operational details. It is a critical component of HUMINT.

Encryption: The method by which information is converted into secret codes that hide the information's true meaning. Encryption is widely used in military and intelligence communications to secure sensitive information.

Information Security (InfoSec): The practice of defending information from unauthorized access, use, disclosure, disruption, modification, or destruction. It is a critical aspect of cybersecurity in intelligence operations.

Interagency Collaboration: The cooperative working relationship between various government agencies to achieve a common goal, often seen in intelligence sharing and joint operations involving SDFs and other military or civilian agencies.

National Guard: A reserve military force composed

of National Guard military members or units of each state and the territories, which operates under the dual control of state governments and the federal government, unlike the SDFs that are state-controlled only.

Psychological Operations (PsyOps): Operations intended to convey selected information and indicators to audiences to influence their emotions, motives, objective reasoning, and ultimately the behavior of governments, organizations, groups, and individuals.

Reconnaissance: A mission to obtain information by visual observation or other detection methods, about the activities and resources of an enemy or potential enemy, or to secure data concerning the meteorological, hydrographic, or geographic characteristics of a particular area.

Surveillance: The continuous observation of a place, person, group, or ongoing activity to gather information. This can be achieved through electronic monitoring, aerial reconnaissance, or human operatives.

Tactical Intelligence: Intelligence that is required for planning and conducting tactical operations at the battalion level and below. It is focused on the current and near-future activities of the adversary and the operational environment.

Threat Assessment: The identification and evaluation of potential threats to national security, public safety, or computer and information security. It involves analyzing the capabilities and intentions of adversaries.

Verification: The process of establishing the truth, accuracy, or validity of something. In intelligence operations, verification is crucial to confirm the reliability of gathered information or sources.

www.ingramcontent.com/pod-product-compliance
Lightning Source LLC
Chambersburg PA
CBHW070157230526
45471CB00002B/710